BIKS AND
GUTCHES

BIKS AND GUTCHES

Learning to Inflect English

A GUIDE FOR TEACHING

Marie M. Clay

Published by Heinemann Education, a division of Reed Publishing (NZ) Ltd, 39 Rawene Road, Birkenhead, Auckland, New Zealand. Associated companies, branches and representatives throughout the world.

In the United States: Heinemann, a division of Reed Elsevier, Inc. (USA), 361 Hanover Street, Portsmouth, NH 03801-3912.

ISBN-13: 978-1-86970-600-5 (NZ)
ISBN-10: 1-86970-600-5 (NZ)
© 2007 The Marie Clay Literacy Trust

Biks and Gutches was first published in 1983 in an edition with *Record of Oral Language*.

Library of Congress Cataloguing-in-Publication Data
CIP data is on file with the Library of Congress
ISBN: 0-325-01293-8
ISBN-13: 978-0-325-01293-3
Global ID: E01293

Cover design by Brenda Cantell
Cover illustration and illustrations on pages 16–40 by Sandra Cammell

Printed in China by Nordica

The pronouns 'she' and 'he' have often been used in this text to refer to the teacher and child respectively. Despite a possible charge of sexist bias it makes for clearer, easier reading if such references are consistent.

Contents

Introduction

What to do with this test

Here is a set of questions to use individually with young children as a 'litmus test'. Should you do anything about some English grammar rules this child ignores, or will time correct the problem? The test was designed for a research study but it proved interesting to the children who took part in the study and to the adults who observed them. The assessment is presented here with some suggestions for how it is used by schools, when teachers have questions about the English language skills of young children.

This observation task was modelled on a piece of research conducted in 1958 by Jean Berko and published in a journal of linguistics called *Word*. She demonstrated clearly that children around the age of five to six years were able to use some rules of English grammar like

- adding or deleting plural endings, like 'watch' and 'watches',
- changing verbs to show tense, like 'run' and 'ran',
- changing adjectives like 'old' to 'older' and 'oldest',
- using pronouns appropriately, using 'himself' and not 'hisself',
- showing possession correctly, like 'girl's' and 'their'.

Berko was not asking how much English children knew. She was asking whether, when they encountered new English words, they knew when to apply the correct endings. She used words they would not have heard before, nonsense words, and she found that by five or six years of age children had a surprisingly good control over the rules for inflecting English.

The high scorers knew the rules and they knew about irregular endings for some words, and not putting any endings on other words. The low scorers knew most about the regular rules and the easy-to-learn words. They improved gradually moving along the same paths being taken by the high scorers of the same age, but the journey took them longer.

In the late 1960s I used Berko's approach on a new set of sentences, combining real English words, and nonsense words, administered to three groups of children in New Zealand schools: children from homes and communities where English was spoken; Maori children living in bilingual communities; and immigrant Samoan children living in bilingual communities. They all attended schools where instruction was given only in English. I was interested to see whether the groups were following similar or different paths in language learning and how much progress with learning about inflections each group had made.

The result is not a test of children's control over English. That would require a more complex set of tasks. 'Biks and Gutches' gives a strong indication of how far particular children have come along the path to controlling the language in their reading books. All readers anticipate up-and-coming text, and therefore children who do not control some of the simple rules of grammar (for using verbs, plurals and possessives in their speech) will be slower to solve these simple problems in their reading and in their own attempts to write.

Why use this observation?

Some suggestions can be made for how teachers might use such an assessment of language acquisition.

a) This is an easy-to-administer-and-score task. It looks too simple to be very useful but with it you can easily predict which young children need you to pay more attention to how they use the English language. You can easily select children who need extra help with learning English.

  ⁘ Some children you test will need no extra attention,

  ⁘ others will need closer attention in class to the language of their reading and writing,

  ⁘ and a third group will need huge amounts of individual conversation time for a period as well as careful attention to their reading and writing instruction, until their control over oral English shows marked improvement.

b) Giving this assessment to individual children will help the teacher to become a better judge of how a child's oral language is changing. For some children this observation feeds into the day-by-day instruction the teacher provides.

c) The same items can be used to evaluate whether a new teaching programme you adopt is having any effect. You can capture *change over two points of time.* For example, you could check on change from the beginning to the end of a school term (a few months). You may regroup children according to whether the change had been rapid, average, slow, or non-existent. That would point to teaching that must occur in the next school term.

d) If the school has introduced some new or special instruction, 'Biks and Gutches' could be used to evaluate its effectiveness. Results could point to the rate and kind of change that has occurred as a result of special attention, such as daily shared book experiences, or individual attention for ten minutes a day from a volunteer helper.

e) For children who speak a dialect of English the test can answer questions like this. *Has the children's control over the rules for inflections of the standard dialect increased?* Children usually learn and use both school and 'home' versions of English and they know when to use either version. Sometimes the non-standard usage dominates, and this can have consequences for school assessments in standard English. Comparing the test and retest scores will allow teachers to see the rates of change and any persistent problems.

f) The items were designed for the five- to seven-year-old age group but have been used successfully in research with children up to 10 years.

The choice of items

In selecting items for any measuring instrument in language one has to choose between a comprehensive linguistic survey of all types of instances and a set of selected items which sample only a few items. After preliminary trials using the 62 items charted below, 36 items (regular print) were selected for further evaluation in a pilot study of children from several ethnic groups in Auckland, New Zealand, in 1968.

Plurals	Regular	*girls*	guns	wugs	
		hats	books	biks	
		houses	*pouches*(**x**)	gutches	
	Irregular	men	feet	calves	
	Uninflected	seaweed	*hay*		
Possessive	Nouns and Pronouns	*girl's*	father's	their	
		his	*her*	*mine*	
Pronouns		*you*	*them*	himself	
Noun Agent		painter	climber		
Adjectives		*dirtier*	*dirtiest*		
		happier	happiest		
		older	oldest		
		kwerkier(**x**)	*kwerkiest*(**x**)		
Verbs		*fishing*	*washing*	*writing*	*waiting*
		climbing	opening	bodding	
		climbs	*sits*	*fishes*	
		opens	paints	washes	
		mots	bods	nazzes	
		climbed	*fished*	*waited*	
		washed	opened	painted	bodded
		sat	swept	wrote	
		will paint	will sweep	will naz	

Items were discarded because

- several fell at the same difficulty level,
- some were easy items (in italics),
- most children failed some hard items (in italics followed by x).

    The 36 items identified provide a reliable measuring scale. They test a child's capacity to inflect real words. But although he may have learned each of the real words one by one, he may still not have learned to apply the rule to a new word. The hardest test of rule learning is passed when a child can inflect a nonsense word correctly. Success with nonsense words tells us that the child has some sense that *it is done this way in this language; he probably knows the rule and when not to use it!*

    The nonsense words in this test do not puzzle young children, and this is probably because they hear new words all the time in the language around them and treat the nonsense words as new words.

1 Administration

Preparation

It is important that this test be administered in a natural, conversational tone. Rehearse the items until the sentences are familiar. Practise giving the test to several children of different ages and ability to ensure a smooth administration procedure that is just like talking. A tape recording of the administration will often show up problems in the tester's behaviour which that tester does not notice.

Recording

Make copies of the answer form on page 13. Mark each response in one of three ways:

- ⊹ write down any incorrect response a child gives,
- ⊹ check (✓) the correct ones,
- ⊹ and mark the ones he refuses with ✗.

Administering the items

The child is shown a picture and the tester introduces the items. For example, showing the picture for items 4, 5 and 6 and pointing to it, the tester reads the text and pauses at the gaps for the child to say the word. Note, in the example below, that the tester introduces a minor variation (in italics) to keep a natural conversational tone; this is allowable.

> The children said to the lady 'Open the door'.
> *[And that's what she's doing.]*
>
> 4 The lady is _____ the door.   (opening)
>
> 5 But she is careful when she _____ it.   (opens)
>
> 6 Yesterday she nearly knocked the little girl over
>   when she _____ the door.   (opened)

So the tester omits the critical word, pausing for the child to say the word.

If necessary the tester can lightly articulate the first sound of the response word, 'o____', to stimulate a child's response. Usually the child will say the word and the tester will complete the sentence, and the story.

Record the response given by the child.

In the presentation of nonsense words the child is shown a picture like the one in items 28 and 29. The tester reads:

28 This calf knows how to naz.
Say 'naz'.
What is he doing?
He is nazzing.
Every day he does this.
Every day he _____.   (nazzes)

29 Tomorrow he will do it.
Tomorrow he _____.   (will naz)

Record the response given by the child.

Scoring the items

Give a score of one point for each correct response. Tally and record the total number of correct responses, the child's total assessment score, on the child's individual record form (page 13). The child's total score is also entered on the cumulative record form (page 14).

Biks and Gutches

Name _____   First Check   Date _____   Score 1 _____

Date of Birth _____   Second Check   Date _____   Score 2 _____

                               Third Check   Date _____   Score 3 _____

		1	2	3			1	2	3
1	climber				19	will paint			
2	houses				20	wugs			
3	Father's				21	bods			
4	opening				22	bodded			
5	opens				23	bodding			
6	opened				24	seaweed			
7	himself				25	swept			
8	wrote				26	will sweep			
9	books				27	calves			
10	sat				28	nazzes			
11	biks				29	will naz			
12	gutches				30	oldest			
13	mots				31	older			
14	feet				32	happiest			
15	washes				33	happier			
16	paints				34	men			
17	painted				35	guns			
18	painter				36	their			

Cumulative Record

School, Class, Group _____ Date _____

Name	Score	Name	Score

Total Scores _____ _____

Range Highest to Lowest _____ _____

Median or Middle Score _____ _____

Mean or Average Score _____ _____

2 Biks and Gutches items

A record form for an individual child and a cumulative record for building up the range of scores typically found in a class or school are included on pages 13 and 14.

Climb the tree

This boy says, 'Watch me climb the tree.'
What is he doing? Yes, climbing the tree.
He is careful when he climbs.

1 He is a good _____ .   (climber)*

*(Accept 'boy'; re-administer, stressing 'cl')

The tree house

These children know how to build a house in a tree.

2 Children like to build lots of ＿＿＿＿＿ in trees.　　　　(houses)

3 The ladder belongs to Father.
Whose ladder is it?
It is ＿＿＿＿ ladder.　　　　　　　　　　(Father's)

Open the door

The children said to the lady, 'Open the door.'

4 The lady is _____ the door. (opening)

5 But she is careful when she _____ it. (opens)

6 Yesterday she nearly knocked the little girl over
when she _____ the door. (opened)

Write your name

This boy can write his name on paper.

7 He can write his name all by _____ .   (himself)

8 Yesterday he did the same thing. Yesterday he
_____ his name.   (wrote)

9 The boy has this book and this book.
He has two _____ .   (books)

10 All the children in this school sit on the floor.
They did the same thing yesterday.
Yesterday they all _____ on the floor.   (sat)

Biks and gutches

11 This is a bik and here is another bik.

There are two _____ .   (biks)

12 There is a gutch and here is another gutch.
There are two _____ .   (gutches)

Mot the ball

13 The big girl can mot the ball with her foot.

Say 'mot'.

What does she do?

She _____ the ball.   (mots)

14 When the ball rolls very fast she can stop it

with both her *(pointing at both feet)* _____ .   (feet)

28

Wash the car

15 You have to wash a car when it gets dirty.

This lady often does this.

This lady often _____ her car.   (washes)

Paint a picture

16 Peter is painting.

He is happy when he _____ .   (paints)

17 Yesterday he did this.

Yesterday he _____ .   (painted)

18 I call him a happy little _____ .   (painter) *

19 Tomorrow he'll do it again.

Tomorrow he _____ .   (will paint)

20 He might paint a wug.

Say 'wug'.

He might even paint two _____ .   (wugs)

(Accept 'boy'; re-administer, stressing 'p')

Bod the seaweed

21 These boats have been out to gather seaweed.
They have to bod the seaweed into big heaps.
Say 'bod'.
Everyone does this.
This man does this.
This man _____ the seaweed.   (bods)

22 Yesterday they _____ the seaweed on to   (bodded)
boats like this.

23 This man is not _____ his seaweed   (bodding)
into a big heap.

24 They get lots and lots of _____ .   (seaweed)

34

Sweep the street

25 Did you ever see people sweep the street?
All these ladies sweep the streets.
Yesterday they did the same thing.
Yesterday they _____ the streets.   (swept)

26 And tomorrow I think they _____   (will sweep)
the street again.

Calves naz

27 This is a calf and here are lots of _____ .   (calves)

28 This calf knows how to naz.

Say 'naz'.

What is he doing?

He is nazzing.

Every day he does this.

Every day he _____ .   (nazzes)

29 Tomorrow he will do it.

Tomorrow he _____ .   (will naz)

Happy people

30 This lady is old.

No one is as old as her.

She is the _____ one.   (oldest)

31 Is the girl as old as the lady?

I think the lady is _____ than the girl.   (older)

32 These people have happy faces.

This one is happy. This one is very happy.

And this one is very, very happy.

The last one seems to be the _____ one.   (happiest)

33 I think this one is happy but I think
that this one is very happy.

I think this one is _____ than that one.   (happier)

Men and guns

34 This is a man and here is another man.

There are two _____ .   (men)

35 This man has a gun, and this man has a gun.

They have two _____ .   (guns)

36 This man put his gun away and this man
put his gun away.

They both put _____ guns away.   (their) *

(Accept 'the' and ask 'Whose guns?')

3 How can we use the assessment results?

After the first study, records were available from 320 children from 10 Auckland schools. I decided to break this large sample into two research groups (with random assignment). So the analysis of results was completed twice for two independent samples. In each sample there were four boys and four girls at each age level (5:0, 5:6, 6:0, 6:6, and 7:0), a total of 40 children in each of four language groups (40 x 4 x 2 = 320).

The question in that first research was 'What changes do we see in children between five and seven years in their ability to use rules for English inflections?'

- ✤ Did we get the same results on both samples?
- ✤ Did favourable opportunities to learn English affect the scoring of the two English groups?
- ✤ Did the two bilingual groups differ from the monolingual groups in

   a) the level of scoring and

   b) the changes that occurred?
- ✤ Did the Maori and Samoan groups differ from each other in

   a) the level of scoring and

   b) the changes that occurred?

The research findings inform procedures for using the assessment results to interpret both school and individual performance and needs.

To make use of information collected by the school

Schools in different geographical regions will probably find that scores vary, so 'national norms' would not be very useful. Schools are recommended to select from three options.

- ✤ **School-based norms** It would be a good idea for any particular school or group (say, the seven-year-olds) to keep a record of the range of scores typically attained by the children they work with, and to determine what is high, average and low scoring within a particular age group in their community. Scores change quite rapidly between five and seven years.
- ✤ **Change over time** Test scores from this assessment provide a useful indicator of one (limited) aspect of language development. And the task is good enough to warrant retesting after a period of time (say, six months) to find out how much change has occurred. Average rates of change for different language groups can be calculated.

Adjustments to the instructional programme could follow, a kind of fine-tuning, and further monitoring could be planned. However, schools are advised to keep to a standard form of the measuring instrument. It is unhelpful to be measuring in inches one year and centimetres the next.

✢ **Calculate group means** Mean scores for age groups 5:0, 6:0, 7:0, 8:0, 9:0 and 10:0 years were calculated in two independent studies (Clay, 1974; Presland, 1973) and are presented in Table 4. But standard deviations around those means will probably vary considerably in size, from group to group. It would be more desirable to build up local school norms over three years than to compare scores with these particular research groups.

To make use of information from one child's test

1. This test is administered to individual children and the total assessment score provides teachers with guidance as to the placement of the individual child in relation to other children. The child may be making fast progress, average progress, or slow progress.

   In Tables 1, 2 and 3, the first column shows the number of errors made (for example 10 out of 40 got 'climb-er' wrong in the Average English group, 16 in the Maori group, and 21 in the Samoan group).

   Easy-to-learn inflections are towards the top of the table. Hard-to-learn items are towards the end of the table, where three quarters of the Average English group, and nine tenths of the two bilingual groups failed items.

   Aim to give more support to the low scorers and bring them close to the average before you withdraw special attention.

2. Subsequent administrations six months or a year apart would allow teachers to judge whether the instruction they are providing helped to close any initial gap between the child and his average classmates.

3. From the child's results, teachers can easily choose an inflection rule or a couple of irregular forms for special attention to work on immediately. Other problems can be left until later.

   Make a copy of the most appropriate table of errors (for either Average English children, or Maori children who are monolingual in English but hear Maori in their communities, and for Samoan children who speak two languages). Mark the errors made by a particular child on the most appropriate table of the three. Extra attention, emphasis or opportunity to increase his control can then be part of some individual attention given by the teacher.

   A list of easy items on which children made no errors is given in Table 1 and the items are not repeated in the other tables. Although children found these easy, the items are retained in the test to make the administration run smoothly.

No. of Errors	Plurals	3rd Person Sing. Verb Present	Verb: Simple Past	Present Participle	Future	Pronouns, Possessives, Adjectives
Table 1 — The Difficulty Order for Inflections for the Average English Group (N = 40)						
Type of Inflection						
0 Easy items	girls, hats	climb, sit, fish, sweep, wait, write	climb, fish wait, wash	climb, fish, wash, wait, write		mine, her, you, his, them, dirty
2	gun-s					
3						father's
4	book-s	paint-s				
5	bik-s					
6	feet	open-s				
7	houses					
8	seaweed					their
9						old-est
10	climb-er					
11	wug-s		open-ed			
12		wash-es		open-ing		old-er
13		mot-s				happi-est
14		bod-s				
15	men				will naz	
16			sat		will sweep	
17			paint-ed		will paint	
18				bod-ding		himself
21	paint-er	naz-zes				
21	cal-ves					
25			swept			
26	gutch-es					
28						happi-er
29			wrote			
30			bod-ded			

More about 'reading' the tables

Table 1 arranges the features tested in the difficulty order that was found for the Average English group. The first column shows the number of errors made. Classes of words have been placed in separate columns across the table. The easy items are grouped at the top of the page and are not repeated in subsequent tables.

The plural phoneme /s/ or /z/ is relatively easy and so is the possessive 'father's'. The present tense of the third person singular verb is also relatively easy, 'paints', 'opens'; it requires only the addition of the same /s/ or /z/ phoneme. This rule can be generalised to nonsense words with relative ease, 'bods', 'mots'.

The third way of forming the plural in English /z/ in 'houses' was more difficult and so was the phonologically similar verb form 'washes'. When children were required to apply these rules to nonsense nouns or verbs the items were among the most difficult in the test, 'gutches', 'nazzes'.

The present participle and the simple past tense of regular verbs were easier to apply to real words, 'opening', 'opened', than to nonsense words, 'bodding', 'bodded'. (The relative difficulty of 'opened' and 'opening' was the reverse of what would be expected from other research and this is perhaps due to a phonological feature of the word 'opening', the two unstressed syllables.) Two very difficult items are the irregular past tense verbs 'wrote' and 'swept'. The future tense was of moderate difficulty. The two pronoun items suggest a range of difficulty within this class of item. The superlative form of the adjective is easier than the comparative form.

It has been suggested that children may learn a dialect from their parents that has its own rules. For example, it is an observation of teachers that Maori children seem to use the inflections of English in flexible ways rather than be constrained by the restriction rules of English morphology. One might expect to find systematic differences in the error patterns of Maori children when compared with children speaking a standard dialect. This was not indicated by the research results. The Maori group made slightly higher error scores and there were slight variations in the order of difficulty (particularly for irregular plurals). Table 2 shows a sequence of learning very similar to that in Table 1.

The bilingual status of 75 percent of the urban Samoan Group was established (Clay, 1971) so we might expect that a viable hypothesis would be that rules from the mother-tongue, Samoan, might create interference with the acquisition and use of English morphological rules and alter the difficulty sequence for Samoan children. The error scores of this group were very high (Table 3) but the order of difficulty is again similar to that of the Average English children.

No. of Errors	Plurals	3rd Person Sing. Verbs Present	Verb: Simple Past	Present Participle	Future	Pronouns, Possessives, Adjectives

Table 2 — The Difficulty Order for Inflections for the Maori Group (N = 40)

Type of Inflection

No. of Errors	Plurals	3rd Person Sing. Verbs Present	Verb: Simple Past	Present Participle	Future	Pronouns, Possessives, Adjectives
4	gun-s					
6	book-s					
8	bik-s					their
9						father's
13		paint-s				
14	seaweed	open-s	open-ed			
15				open-ing		
16	climb-er					old-est
18	feet	bod-s				
21	wug-s	mot-s		bod-ding	will paint	happi-est
22	houses				will naz	old-er
23	cal-ves		paint-ed			
23			sat			
27						himself
28					will sweep	
29	men	wash-es				
30	paint-er					
34						
35		naz-zes	wrote			happi-er
35			bod-ded			
36	gutch-es		swept			

Table 3 — The Difficulty Order for Inflections for the Samoan Group (N = 40)						
Type of Inflection						
No. of Errors	Plurals	3rd Person Sing. Verb Present	Verb: Simple Past	Present Participle	Future	Pronouns, Possessives, Adjectives
12	book-s					
14	gun-s					
15						their
17	seaweed		open-ed			
20						father's
21	climb-er	paint-s				old-est
22	feet					
23				open-ing	will naz	happi-est
24	bik-s					
25	houses	open-s	sat		will paint	old-er
26	paint-er			bod-ding		
27	wug-s	mot-s				himself
28		bod-s				
30			paint-ed		will sweep	
32	men					
32	cal-ves					
33						happi-er
35		wash-es				
37			wrote			
37		naz-zes	swept			
37			bod-ded			
38	gutch-es					

The items as arranged in Tables 1–3 cannot be interpreted as an order of acquisition because each table reports the pooled scores of children who were between five and seven years. Whether the difficulty order reported is related to a difficulty sequence for acquisition would have to be tested on longitudinal data.

Development after seven years of age is reported by Presland (1973) who applied the same test to English, Maori and Samoan children at 8:0, 9:0 and 10:0 years using 90 children from 12 Auckland schools. His mean scores showed an improvement with age for all three groups, with a fairly satisfactory level of scoring by the urban Maori and urban Samoan groups from 9:0 years onwards on the real word items. Yet at 10:0 years both the Maori and Samoan mean scores were lower than those of the Average English children of 8:0 years; that is, an achievement lag still existed in this limited aspect of language development (Table 4).

Table 4 — Mean Inflection Test Scores in Clay and Presland Studies for Three Language Groups

	Clay			Presland		
Age	5:0	6:0	7:0	8:0	9:0	10:0
Average English	19.6	21.9	29.6	32.9	33.3	35.0
Maori	9.8	14.9	23.2	22.1	28.3	28.6
Samoan	6.1	11.2	19.9	20.4	29.4	30.5

How research and theory contribute to understanding individual scores

The questions posed can be said to test children's control over the inflections of English (pages 15–41). Results from three different samples of New Zealand children are reported in three error tables for five- to seven-year-olds.

The very young child who has begun to combine words into phrases begins to use inflections. He has little difficulty operating as if he had some general notion of the rules that govern word changes (Dale, 1972). He is able to learn a pattern and he applies it as generally as possible, treating irregular examples as if they were regular. He says 'We goed to town', using a past tense ending which matches 'showed' and 'mowed'. At times he extends the use of a pattern beyond acceptable limits. At other times he tries to match the patterns used by people around him. There is a steady improvement in his control of the rules for inflecting words towards mastery of the most difficult by about 12 years (Selby, 1972).

The evidence that children's use of inflections is guided by rules was provided by Berko (1958) because her subjects were able to inflect nonsense words in ways which agreed with the inflection rules of English. Kirk and McCarthy (1966) provided statistical evidence from 700 children aged 2:6 to 9:0 that scores on a test of inflections increased regularly with age and were related to many other types of oral language scores.

There is clear evidence from research that the child's control over the inflections of English changes as experience with language accumulates. Simple plurals, possessives and the progressive present tense verbs reach perfect control in the 5:0- to 7:0-year age range. At first children achieve correct performance with the most regular forms which have the fewest variants and only after more experience do they control the irregular and infrequent variants or instances.

Besides those available research reports there is also theoretical discussion about the learning of inflections in the language acquisition literature. Young children discover regularities. In their speech they make the irregular regular, as in 'breaked' and 'eated', and 'broked' and 'ated'. We hear plural errors like 'mans', 'foots', 'tooths', and 'mouses'. In English there is an obligatory 's' ending on the third person singular verb ('I come', 'you come' but 'she comes') but three common verbs do not take the obligatory 's' — 'have', 'do', and 'to be'. You can hear little children applying the general rule to all three exceptions.

> He just haves a cold.
> She doos what her mother tells her.
> No, she be's bad, then she be's good, okay?

We hear young children struggling with comparatives and superlatives, saying 'specialer' and 'powerfullest'. The behaviour appears to be governed by an implicit learning of some rules.

Children's speech errors make engaging anecdotes in poetry, novels, television features, and websites for parents. But we may have a lot more to learn about such errors. Those comments come from Steven Pinker's discussion of how children's errors may help us to untangle one of the thickest knots in the science of nature and nurture.

> When a child says 'bleeded', builded', and 'singed', every bit of every word has been learned, including the past-tense suffix -ed. The very existence of the errors comes from a process of learning that is as yet incomplete: the mastery of the irregular forms 'bled' and 'sang'. (Pinker, 1999, page 233)

His argument is not about how to get the child to inflect words correctly. It is more important than that. He claims that preschoolers' brains work in two ways with language.

1. One way to work on language is to store the regular examples together and simply make a rule to cover that regularity. There is great economy in this. The speaker can apply the new rule to a wide range of words or sentences. The rule will begin to fit with others in the child's grammatical system. He may then use the rule and not have to remember all the individual items. Just apply the rule when a likely word turns up.

2. The second way is to work on irregular words. When you hear or see an irregular word, capture it and store it with similar patterns. That means that for special instances of irregularity Pinker suggests that the brain creates special categories.

He concludes that the brain constructs regular forms from rules, and uses memory for the irregular forms. You do not have to direct little brains to handle the regularities of language, just point up the recurrence of 'an old friend'. Irregular forms were generated by rules way back in linguistic history but the rules died long ago.

If the child is being schooled in English as a second language he will need a huge quantity of make-up opportunities to create the rule-governed base to language that the mother-tongue child already has. What is causing the limitations of that child's progress? Does he learn slowly? Or could it be that your programme deprives him of the opportunities he needs to form those regular rules? Are you providing opportunities to use/hear the second language?

When we look specifically at the learning of rules for adding inflections to English words, the rate and direction of change in those results follow the same pattern. The average scores for the four language groups at each age level on inflections were in the same order as those for the total language scores for the four different assessments of language. At 10 years of age the Samoan child has not reached the average level of the Average English child of eight years.

The fact that the acquisition sequence is the same for all groups supports my proposition that it is features of the English language that determine the acquisition sequence rather than interference between any two languages. What is easy and what is difficult is much the same for all the children but when they face a particular learning challenge difficulty depends on what they have learned so far.

What is needed is not a different sequence of language lessons but greater English-language enrichment beginning in the preschool years. This simple and easy-to-administer assessment identifies the school entrants who require energetic and intensive extra opportunities to enrich and extend their use of English language. This is not a need to *hear* more English: it is more *a need to use more English*. School does not allow for the quantity of talking (and linking) that children need to do.

Regular and commonly used inflections are mastered before complex and infrequently used forms. It is obvious that children learn regular rules before irregular instances because we notice the 'errors' in their everyday speech.

The research literature shows that some types of inflections are easy to learn and others are more difficult. The types of inflection which prove easy or difficult to inflect were found to be close to identical in three language groups. The numbers of children in the four language groups who failed items differed, but the order of challenge or difficulty of the items in three tables listing the 36 items in this assessment place the items (approximately) in the same order of difficulty.

The general picture emerging from the early studies is that children acquire a knowledge of some morphological rules, beginning with inflections or verb tense changes which are regular and commonly used, and gradually perfect that knowledge and add to it those forms that are more complex and infrequently used.

Maori and Samoan children who enter school with a less-developed knowledge followed a pattern of acquisition along similar lines to that of English-only children.

Appendix: The replicated research study

Using four different tests of language learning

In a large study of language and literacy, a language learning score was obtained from four different tests of oral English, namely articulation, vocabulary, sentence repetition, *and this test of inflections*. Results were reported in the *New Zealand Journal of Educational Studies* in 1970.

The total sample of 320 children was divided randomly into two equivalent samples and the hypotheses were tested twice in two parallel studies. Each of the samples included children of four distinct language groups. For this discussion, the focus will be review of the results for three subgroups studied: a group of average children from English-speaking homes, a second group of English-speaking Maori children from bilingual communities, and a third group of Samoan-speaking children from bilingual communities. (The fourth group, English-speaking children from educationally advantaged families, is not relevant to this report.) On the basis of their language learning scores, the three subgroups were ranked in the same order at five, six, and seven years of age, in both Sample 1 and Sample 2. The resulting ranking was average English speaking children, English-speaking Maori children, and Samoan-speaking children.

A study of 90 children (Presland, 1973) from the same language groups but aged eight, nine and 10 years extended the inquiry to older children. Mean scores continued to demonstrate differences between all three groups with one exception. By 10 years the Samoan-speaking group had drawn slightly ahead of the English-speaking Maori group.

The results of these investigations revealed that language achievement at school entry for the three groups of children studied was spread across a wide range of scores when they began school. Each sub-group made large gains in language learning in the first two years of school, and between eight and 10 years. In one sense we could say that all children ran a good race, and the gaps between the monolingual and bilingual groups were being reduced. However, a detectable difference in language learning found at school entrance continued to place them at a slight disadvantage. Schools could do much more to accelerate the language learning of the Maori and Samoan children in the language of instruction earlier in their school careers.

The four language groups had different degrees of control over the inflection rules of English, but within each group the patterns of difficulties were similar. They appear to be determined more by factors within the English language, such as frequency, regularity or phonemic shape, than by factors within the children such as interference from features or rules of another dialect or language.

None of the groups showed particular and different patterns of responding but this does not in itself imply that special instruction was not needed. What it does suggest is that a similar teaching sequence might apply to many language groups. One research study (Osser, Wang and Zaid, 1969) suggested a procedure for achieving effective learning with inflections. While intuitive judgement might lead teachers to go from the singular to the plural, or uninflected to inflected, or present to past, the Osser et al. research presents strong evidence that for the best results the teacher's examples should be the 'hard' one or inflected example and the child's response the 'easier' of the two paired items, the uninflected example.

Descriptive research of this kind can yield important information about regularities in acquisition.

- Such data is helpful for teachers in understanding what a child can already do.
- Seeing a particular child's achievement in the context of what we know about the general patterns of acquisition can assist teachers in deciding what to emphasise next in a learning programme.

References

Berko, Jean. The child's learning of English morphology. *Word.* 1958, 14: 150–77.

Clay, Marie M. Language skills: a comparison of Maori, Samoan and Pakeha children aged five to seven years. *New Zealand Journal of Educational Studies.* 1970, 5, 2: 153–62.

———. The Polynesian language skills of Maori and Samoan school entrants. *International Journal of Psychology.* 1971, 6, 2: 135–45.

———. The development of morphological rules in children of differing language backgrounds. *New Zealand Journal of Educational Studies.* 1974, 9, 2: 113–21.

———. Learning to inflect English words. *Regional English Language Centre Journal,* 1975, 6, 11: 33–42.

Dale, P.S. *Language Development: Structure and Function.* Hinsdale, Illinois: The Dryden Press, 1972.

Kirk, S.A. and McCarthy, J.J. The Illinois Test of Psycholinguistic Abilities. *American Journal of Mental Deficiency.* 1966, 399–412.

Osser, H., Wang, M.D. and Zaid, F. The young child's ability to imitate and comprehend speech: a comparison of two sub-cultural groups. *Child Development.* 1969, 40: 1063–75.

Pinker, S. *Words and Pictures.* London: A Phoenix paperback, 1999.

Presland, I.V. Inflection skills: a comparison between Maori, Samoan and English children aged eight to ten years. Unpublished Dip. Ed. thesis, University of Auckland Library, 1973.

Selby, S. The development of morphological rules in children. *British Journal of Educational Psychology.* 1972, 42, 5: 293–99.